80 Internet
Mini-Scavenger Hunts

**Reproducible Activity Cards That Help Kids Build
Internet Research Skills as They Find Fascinating Facts
in Social Studies, Science, Math, and Language Arts**

by Michelle Robinette

S C H O L A S T I C
PROFESSIONAL BOOKS

NEW YORK • TORONTO • LONDON • AUCKLAND • SYDNEY
MEXICO CITY • NEW DELHI • HONG KONG • BUENOS AIRES

Cover design by Norma Ortiz
Interior design by Solutions by Design, Inc.
Illustrations by Mike Moran

ISBN 0-439-31754-1

Copyright © 2003 by Scholastic Inc.
All rights reserved. Printed in the U.S.A

4 5 6 7 8 9 10   40   08 07 06 05

CONTENTS

Introduction 4

Social Studies 7

Science 17

Math 27

Language Arts 37

INTRODUCTION

Doing research today is not quite the same as doing research 20 years ago. Back then, the best place to find information was in the library—you walked up to the reference section and pulled out an encyclopedia, or approached the librarian for assistance. Today, we have the Internet, a vast network of computers filled with seemingly endless amounts of information—and not all of it very reliable. How can we help students sort through this barrage of information? By teaching them to navigate—one step at a time.

That's what this book is all about: building Internet research skills by doing a little bit at a time. Each of the 80 Internet mini-scavenger hunts in this book contains two to five questions that students can find the answers to in about 10 minutes or less.

Using This Book

80 Internet Mini-Scavenger Hunts is divided into four sections: social studies, science, math, and language arts. There are 20 "cards" for each of the content areas. In front of the cards, you'll find a short introduction to the topic, the URL or site address, and one to four questions, plus a challenge question. The back of the card provides the answers to all the questions. You can make double-sided copies of the cards on cardstock, or just copy the question side and keep the answers separate. Cut apart the cards and store them in a small box next to your computer. Then send students on a mini-scavenger hunt during choice time or when they finish their work early.

Accessing the Web Sites

Although we have checked and double-checked all the URLs in this book, please be sure to preview each site before sending students to the computer. You'll want to make sure that the site hasn't changed and that the material is appropriate for your students. In addition, you can familiarize yourself with the site's contents so you're able to help students navigate through the site efficiently.

For easy access to the Web sites, you can bookmark the sites (or add them to your favorites) and organize them into a folder for students to use. You can also go to our own Web site at:

http://www.scholastic.com/profbooks/easyinternet/index.htm

Simply click on the book cover of *80 Internet Mini-Scavenger Hunts* to enter a page with links to all the sites listed in this book. Then click on the URL to automatically go to that Web site. We will be updating the links on our site quite regularly, so if any of the URLs printed on this book do change, you can always find an alternative at our Web site.

Enjoy the hunt!

Tips for a Successful Hunt

The activities in this book are designed so students can work independently, either individually or in small groups. To help students get the most out of their time online, share with them these helpful tips before they embark on their Internet scavenger hunts:

1.

Read the activity card carefully before going to the computer. This way, students will know ahead of time what kind of information they need to find. You may want to go over the activity as a class to discuss any questions students may have.

2.

Browse through the Web site for relevant information. Tell students that they don't have to read everything on the site. They can just skim through until they find the information they need. Have them refer back to their activity card regularly so they know what to look for next.

3.

Explore the various links on the page to get more information. In some Web sites, certain pictures or words within the text may be highlighted or underlined. Clicking on these links usually opens another page that gives a more in-depth explanation of the word or phrase. (Note: As much as possible, we've tried to avoid Web sites with advertisements. However, some very useful sites do feature them. Caution students against clicking on any ads that may appear on a Web site.)

4.

Use the commands Find or Find Again under the Edit toolbar to help search for a particular word on the Web page. For example, if students are looking for the definition of "capitalism," they could quickly look for the word in the Web page by using the command Find.

SOCIAL STUDIES

On a car ride with your parents, how many times have you asked, "Are we there yet?" Now you can figure out how many miles you'll be traveling all by yourself! But first, go to the following Web site to find the distance between the cities below:

How Far Is It?

http://www.indo.com/distance

1. Find the distance between Seattle, Washington, and New York, New York.
2. Find the distance between Dallas, Texas, and Atlanta, Georgia.
3. Find the distance between your hometown and your favorite destination.

CHALLENGE: Which is longer—a mile or a kilometer?

Card #2

SOCIAL STUDIES

You just won a free trip to Mexico! Spend some time researching the country to prepare for your journey. Visit this Web site, then answer the questions below:

Meet Mexico

http://www.demon.co.uk/mexuk/meet_mex/index.htm

1. What does the word Olmec mean?
2. What is the Mexican unit of currency?
3. What language is spoken in Mexico?

CHALLENGE: Write a letter to your best friend describing your first day in Mexico. Be sure to include information about the food you ate, the sites you visited, the weather, and the people.

Card #4

SOCIAL STUDIES

Have you ever looked at your state flag and wondered, "Why did they use those colors?" or "What does that symbol mean?" Go to this site to get the scoop on your own state flag, then find the answers to the questions below:

USA State Flags and Symbols

http://www.imagesoft.net/flags/usstate1.html

1. What do the bear and the star represent on California's state flag?
2. Why is there a palmetto tree on South Carolina's state flag?
3. What animal appears in the center of Wyoming's state flag?

CHALLENGE: How many stars were on the United States flag in 1863?

Card #1

SOCIAL STUDIES

Even though Canada is our next-door neighbor (it borders the United States to the north), you probably don't know much about this country or its people. Visit this site to learn more about Canada, then answer the questions below:

The World Factbook: Canada

http://www.odci.gov/cia/publications/factbook/geos/ca.html

1. What title is given to Canada's head of government?
2. When do Canadians celebrate their independence?
3. How many provinces and territories make up Canada?

CHALLENGE: What are the two official languages of Canada?

Card #3

SOCIAL STUDIES — Card #4

Answers:

1. "The dweller in the land of rubber"
2. Peso
3. Spanish

CHALLENGE: Answers will vary.

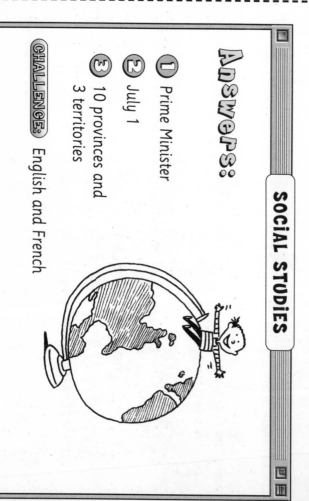

SOCIAL STUDIES — Card #2

Answers:

1. 2,413 miles
2. 717 miles
3. Answers will vary.

CHALLENGE: A mile

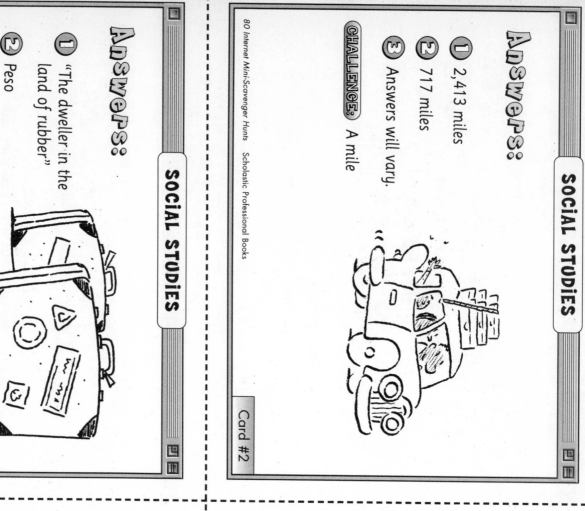

SOCIAL STUDIES — Card #3

Answers:

1. Prime Minister
2. July 1
3. 10 provinces and 3 territories

CHALLENGE: English and French

SOCIAL STUDIES — Card #1

Answers:

1. The bear symbolizes great strength and the star refers to the Lone Star of Texas.
2. The palmetto tree represents Col. William Moultrie's heroic defense of the palmetto-log fort on Sullivan's Island against a British fleet attack.
3. A bison

CHALLENGE: 35

SOCIAL STUDIES

A map is very useful for figuring out where you are or finding a particular place. But did you know that maps offer a wealth of information other than location? Learn more about this invaluable tool by visiting the following site:

Maps and Globes

http://pittsford.monroe.edu/jefferson/calfieri/maps&globes/mapsglobesframe.html

1. What do historical maps show?
2. Define the term latitude.
3. What kind of map is associated with governments?

CHALLENGE: Create a map of your school. Make sure you include a key or legend.

Card #6

SOCIAL STUDIES

The Liberty Bell rang proudly at the first public reading of the Declaration of Independence on July 8, 1776 (not on July 4). Learn more about this enduring American symbol at the following site and answer the questions below:

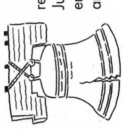

Liberty Bell Facts

http://home.att.net/~tom.jordan/LibertyBell/history/bellfacts.htm

1. What was the first name given to the Liberty Bell?
2. How old was the bell when it was first called the Liberty Bell?
3. What is the most popular date given for when the famous crack in the Liberty Bell occurred?

CHALLENGE: What is the current weight of the Liberty Bell?

Card #8

SOCIAL STUDIES

Have you wondered what it might have been like to live in ancient times? What did cities around the world look like in the past? Click on the various images at the site below to learn more about ancient civilizations:

World Map of Ancient Civilizations

http://www.taisei.co.jp/cg_e/ancient_world/world_map.html

1. What was the capital of the Aztec Empire in 1300 A.D.?
2. What did the Mongols call themselves?
3. How were houses in ancient Venice designed and why?

CHALLENGE: What Chinese city did Marco Polo visit to meet Khublai Khan?

Card #5

SOCIAL STUDIES

Jamestown, Virginia, was the first permanent English settlement in the United States. How did Jamestown get its start? What difficulties did its colonists face? Browse through this site to find out:

A Brief History of Jamestown, Virginia

http://www.historian.org/local/jamstwnva.htm#aa2

1. How did the colonists contribute to the failure of Jamestown?
2. What crop turned Jamestown into an economic success?
3. What name did Pocahontas take after converting to Christianity?

CHALLENGE: What three objectives did King James give the London Company when he sent them to the New World?

Card #7

SOCIAL STUDIES — Card #6

Answers:

1. How a place's geography has changed over time in relation to its history

2. A measurement of how far north or south a place is from the equator

3. Political map

CHALLENGE: Answers will vary.

SOCIAL STUDIES — Card #8

Answers:

1. The State House Bell

2. 86 years old

3. 1835, while tolling for the funeral of Chief Justice John Marshall

CHALLENGE: 2,055 lbs

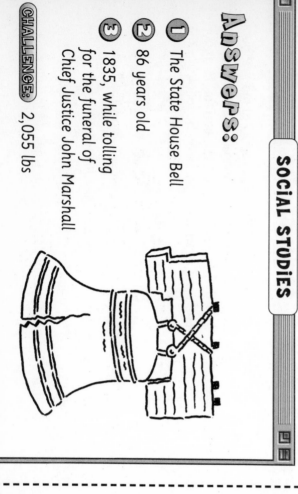

SOCIAL STUDIES — Card #5

Answers:

1. Tenochtitlan

2. "People of the plains"

3. The entrance of a house was designed so that visitors could go directly from their boats into the house.

CHALLENGE: Dadu (or Beijing)

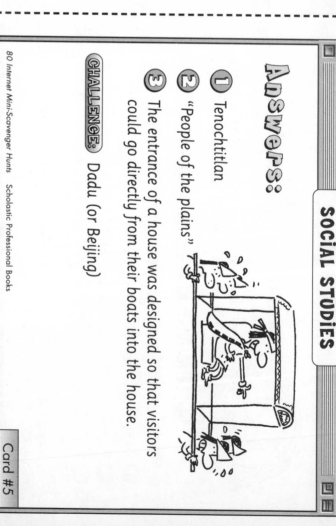

SOCIAL STUDIES — Card #7

Answers:

1. The colonists were "gentlemen adventurers," who didn't know how to work and refused to cooperate among themselves and with the natives.

2. Tobacco

3. Rebecca

CHALLENGE: Find gold, find a route to the South Seas, and find the lost colony of Roanoke

What does it take to become President of the United States of America? Who are the men who have held this office? Learn more about our presidents and their lives at the following Web site:

The American Presidents

http://www.americanpresident.org/presbios/presbios.htm

1) During what years did George Washington serve in office?

2) What was William H. Harrison's claim to fame as President of the United States? How long was he in office?

3) What role did Ulysses S. Grant play in the Civil War?

CHALLENGE: Who issued the Emancipation Proclamation?

Card #9

Many of our nation's rivers are protected by the National Wild and Scenic Rivers System. Explore the following site to learn how and why our rivers are being protected:

Wild and Scenic Rivers

http://www.nps.gov/rivers

1) According to the Wild and Scenic Rivers Act, what characteristics should a river possess in order to be protected under this act?

2) Which state has the most number of rivers protected by the Wild and Scenic Rivers Act?

3) What four federal agencies are part of the Interagency Wild & Scenic Rivers Coordinating Council?

CHALLENGE: When was the act first passed?

Card #10

There are four major time zones in the United States (not including Hawaii and Alaska), and more than 20 in the world. Learn more about time zones at:

Time Zone Converter

http://www.timezoneconverter.com/cgi-bin/tzc.tzc

1) It is 12:00 P.M. in Denver, Colorado. What time is it in Hong Kong?

2) It is 5:35 P.M. in Anchorage, Alaska. What time is it in Honolulu, Hawaii?

3) It is 6:37 P.M. in London. What time is it in Jerusalem?

CHALLENGE: How many hours difference is there between Honolulu and New York?

Card #11

Do you know the capital of all 50 states? What about the capitals of countries around the world? Visit this site to find the capital cities of the countries listed below:

Capitals.com

http://www.capitals.com

1) What is the capital of the Bahamas?

2) What is the capital of Cambodia?

3) What is the capital of Ecuador?

4) What is the capital of Italy?

CHALLENGE: What are the geographical coordinates of Liberia?

Card #12

Card #10

Answers:

① Rivers should possess scenic, recreational, geologic, fish and wildlife, historic or cultural values.

② Oregon

③ Bureau of Land Management, National Park Service, U.S. Fish and Wildlife Service, and U.S. Forest Service

CHALLENGE: 1968

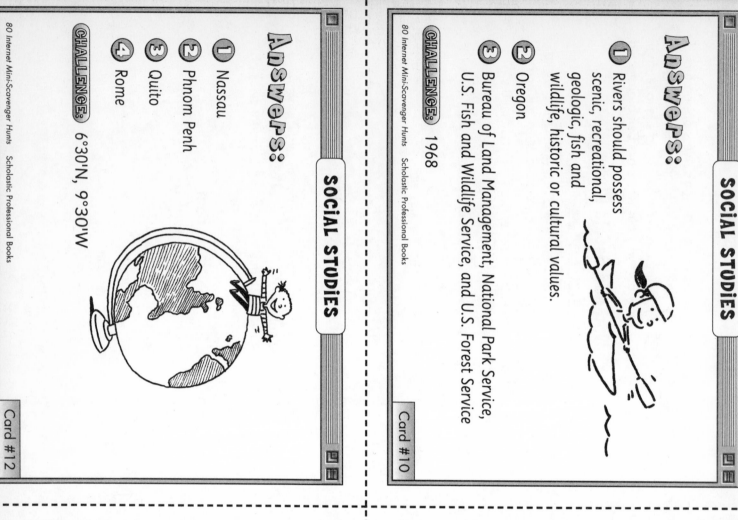

Card #12

Answers:

① Nassau

② Phnom Penh

③ Quito

④ Rome

CHALLENGE: 6°30'N, 9°30'W

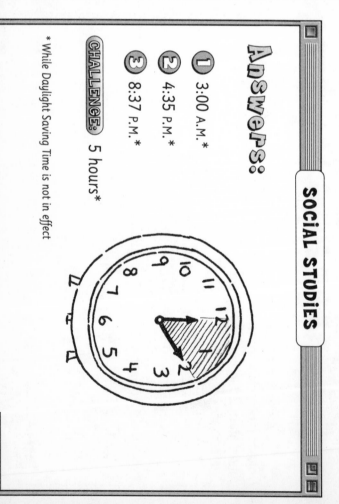

Card #9

Answers:

① 1789–1797

② He was the first president to die in office after serving only one month.

③ Supreme commander

CHALLENGE: Abraham Lincoln

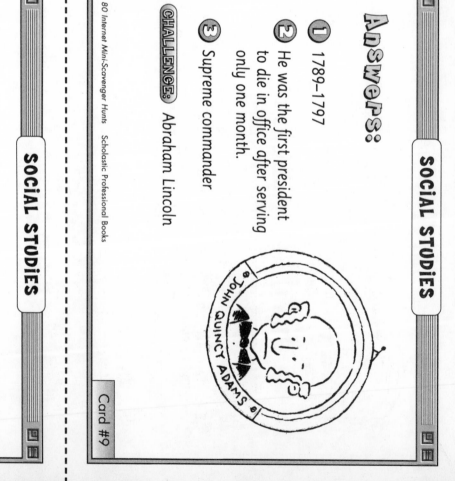

Card #11

Answers:

① 3:00 A.M.*

② 4:35 P.M.*

③ 8:37 P.M.*

CHALLENGE: 5 hours*

* While Daylight Saving Time is not in effect

SOCIAL STUDIES

Did you know that the White House has 35 bathrooms? Take a tour of this presidential home at the following Web site and find the answers to the questions below:

The White House for Kids

http://www.whitehouse.gov/kids/whlife

1. How many floors does the White House have?
2. Who was the first president to live in the White House?
3. How many guests can the State Dining Room hold for dinner or lunch?

CHALLENGE: What is the largest room in the White House?

Card #14

SOCIAL STUDIES

Imagine what it would be like if the northern states waged war against the southern states today. Americans in the 1860s lived through just such a situation. Learn more about the devastating Civil War at:

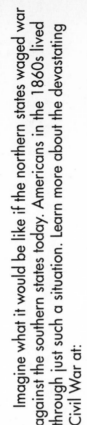

The American Civil War Experience

http://library.thinkquest.org/3055/netscape

1. When was the Battle of Gettysburg fought?
2. When and where did General Robert E. Lee surrender?
3. Who stated, "War is cruelty. There is no use trying to reform it. The crueler it is, the sooner it will be over."

CHALLENGE: Who was President of the Union during the Civil War?

Card #16

SOCIAL STUDIES

What exactly does "daylight saving time" save, and why do we "spring forward" and "fall back" every year? Browse the following Web site to discover about daylight saving time:

About Daylight Saving Time

http://webexhibits.org/daylightsaving

1. Who first conceived the idea of daylight saving time and when?
2. Why do we have daylight saving time?
3. What three U.S. states do not observe daylight saving time?

CHALLENGE: What does the European Union call daylight saving time?

Card #13

SOCIAL STUDIES

Economics may sound like such an intimidating word to some kids. What exactly is it, and why is it important? Visit the following Web site to learn more, then search for the answers to the questions below:

Economics

http://pittsford.monroe.edu/jefferson/calfieri/economics/econmain.html

1. Define the term commerce.
2. What is the difference between socialism and capitalism?
3. What does bankruptcy mean?

CHALLENGE: What do the letters NASDAQ stand for?

Card #15

Card #14

Answers:

1. Six
2. President John Adams
3. 130 guests

CHALLENGE: East Room

Card #16

Answers:

1. July 1 to 3, 1863
2. On April 9, 1865, Lee surrendered at Appomattox.
3. Union General William T. Sherman

CHALLENGE: Abraham Lincoln

Card #13

Answers:

1. Benjamin Franklin first conceived the idea in 1784.
2. It gives us more hours of daylight and it saves energy.
3. Hawaii, Arizona, and the Eastern Time Zone portion of Indiana

CHALLENGE: Summer time

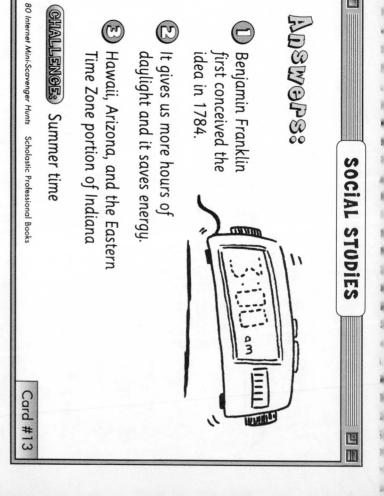

Card #15

Answers:

1. Trade between states and nations
2. Socialism is a system in which the government is in control of the economy, including the production and distribution of goods. In capitalism, there is private or corporate ownership of production and distribution of goods.
3. Bankruptcy means that a person is so deeply in debt that he or she cannot repay his or her loans.

CHALLENGE: National Association of Securities Dealers Automated Quotation System

Throughout our country's history, Native Americans have been treated unfairly. One of the most disgraceful acts against Native Americans was the forced relocation of the Cherokee Indians, also known as the Trail of Tears. Learn more about it at:

The Cherokee Trail of Tears

http://rosecity.net/tears

1. How many miles were the Cherokees forced to walk?
2. When did this journey take place?
3. About how many Cherokee Indians died on this journey?

CHALLENGE: What is the symbol for pain and suffering on the Trail of Tears?

Card #18

Archaeology is the study of artifacts and other remains from the past. But what about maritime archaeology? What do maritime archaeologists study? Embark on an exciting journey under the water by visiting this Web site:

What Is Underwater Archaeology?

http://www.abc.se/~pa/uwa/whatis.htm

1. What do maritime archaeologists study?
2. What was the Vasa and when did it sink?
3. Why are shipwrecks in the Baltic Sea and the Great Lakes better preserved than those in the Atlantic and other salt seas?

CHALLENGE: What is an amphora?

Card #20

Totem poles are an integral part of the Native American culture in the Northwest Pacific. They serve as symbols of a clan or family and as reminders of the family's ancestry. Browse through the following Web site to discover more about totem poles:

Totem Poles: An Exploration

http://users.imag.net/~sry.jkramer/nativetotems/default.html

1. What are totem poles made out of?
2. Where can you find the tallest totem pole still standing today?
3. What does it mean for a totem pole to be "sanctioned"?

CHALLENGE: What does the expression "low man on the totem pole" mean and why is it misleading?

Card #17

Looking for a really cool place? Nothing can be cooler (or should we say colder) than Antarctica! Learn some great stuff about this rarely visited area of our world. Visit this Web site, then answer the questions below:

Glacier Index

http://www.glacier.rice.edu

1. What is the lowest temperature ever recorded in Antarctica?
2. What percentage of the earth's ice does the Antarctic Ice Sheet hold?
3. What are katabatic winds?

CHALLENGE: How does Antarctica affect the Earth's climate?

Card #19

Card #18

Answers:

1. 800 to 1,000 miles

2. Through the winter of 1838 and into early spring of 1839

3. More than 4,000

CHALLENGE: Cherokee rose

Card #20

Answers:

1. They study the past from shipwrecks, as well as sunken dwellings and ports.

2. A Swedish battle galleon, which sank in 1628 on her maiden voyage

3. Ship worms, which feed on wooden wrecks, live only in salty water. The Baltic Sea and the Great Lakes have low salinity.

CHALLENGE: An amphora is a large ceramic container used until the 16th century to store goods.

Card #17

Answers:

1. Cedar trees

2. In Victoria, British Columbia, Canada

3. It is authentically made by Native Americans and blessed by the elders.

CHALLENGE: The expression implies that the low man on the totem pole is the least important or lacks status, but in reality, the most intricate and best-carved figures are placed at the bottom end of the totem pole.

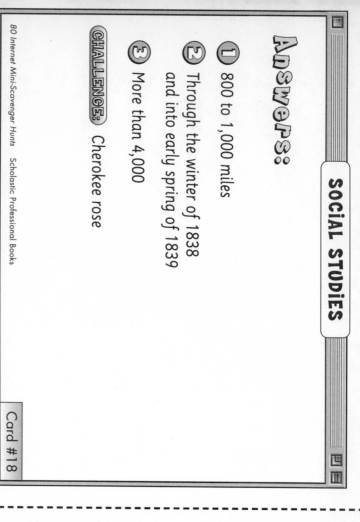

Card #19

Answers:

1. –129°F

2. 91 percent

3. Katabatic winds are the result of dense, cold air blowing down-slope as a result of gravity.

CHALLENGE: Antarctica acts as a global heat sink and helps to control the climate.

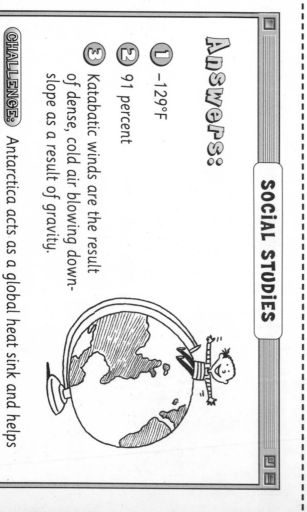

SCIENCE

There are hundreds of active volcanoes around the world—and more and more people are living dangerously near them. Being able to predict when volcanoes might erupt could save many lives. Start your study of volcanoes at this site:

Volcanoes

http://www.learner.org/exhibits/volcanoes

1. How does magma become lava?
2. What are plate boundaries?
3. What are the most common and serious volcanic hazards?

CHALLENGE: What types of tools does a volcanologist use to monitor volcanoes?

Card #1

SCIENCE

The western diamondback rattlesnake is one of the most dangerous snakes in the United States. It's definitely a snake you want to avoid at all costs! Visit this site to learn more about the western diamondback, then find the answers to the questions below:

Western Diamondback Rattlesnake

http://www.wf.net/~snake/rattlesn.htm

1. Where in the United States can you find the western diamondback rattlesnake?
2. What do western diamondbacks eat?
3. How long is the average full-grown western diamondback?

CHALLENGE: How many eggs does the female western diamondback usually lay?

Card #2

SCIENCE

Butterflies are among the most beautiful creatures in the world. And you can attract them to your backyard just by planting certain types of plants. Learn more about butterflies by exploring this site:

The Butterfly Zone

http://www.butterflies.com

1. What type of plant does the yellow sulfur butterfly prefer?
2. Could you find a pearl crescent butterfly on the Pacific coast?
3. How do butterflies identify their favorite plants?

CHALLENGE: What are the stages of the complete life cycle of a butterfly?

Card #3

SCIENCE

Avalanche! How can something as light as snow be so deadly? Find out more about avalanches and their dangers at this site. Then answer the questions below:

Nova Online / Avalanche!

http://www.pbs.org/wgbh/nova/avalanche/textindex.html

1. What two elements are necessary for a snow slide?
2. How many avalanches do scientists estimate occur each year?
3. Which is deadlier in the United States—avalanches or earthquakes?

CHALLENGE: Design a pamphlet instructing people how to predict a possible avalanche and what to do if caught in one.

Card #4

Card #4

SCIENCE

Answers:

1 Snow-covered slope and a trigger

2 1 million

3 Avalanches

CHALLENGE: Answers will vary.

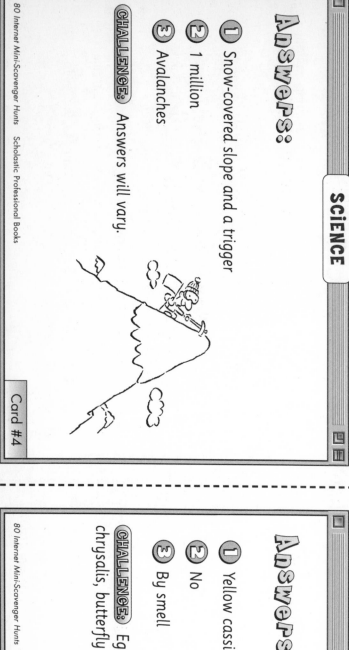

Card #2

SCIENCE

Answers:

1 Southwestern United States

2 Small rodents, rabbits, and birds

3 Around 60 inches long

CHALLENGE: None, they have live births

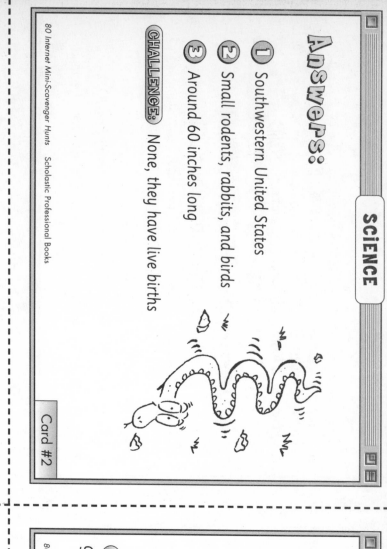

Card #3

SCIENCE

Answers:

1 Yellow cassia

2 No

3 By smell

CHALLENGE: Egg, caterpillar, chrysalis, butterfly

Card #1

SCIENCE

Answers:

1 Magma reaches the surface and becomes lava.

2 Areas where the earth's shifting plates meet or split apart

3 Lava, ash, and debris flows

CHALLENGE: Seismographs, tiltmeters, geodimeters, correlation spectrometers

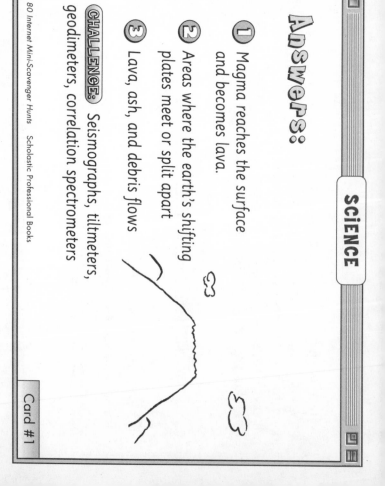

SCIENCE

The universe is truly awe-inspiring, filled with wonders and mysteries. For example, what holds the planets in our solar system around the sun? Why is Earth the only planet with life in our solar system? Find the answers to these and the questions below at the following site:

NASA Kids

http://kids.msfc.nasa.gov

1) What is the diameter of the sun?

2) How many Earth days long is a year on the planet Mercury?

3) What type of scientist studies the atmosphere of planets?

CHALLENGE: What is the heart of a comet called?

Card #6

SCIENCE

The ocean is home to both microscopic plankton and the largest animal in the world, the blue whale. All the plants and animals that live in the ocean work together to create a balanced ecosystem. Learn more about our water world at this site, then find answers to the questions below:

What's It Like Where You Live?

http://mbgnet.mobot.org/salt/index.htm

1) How much of the earth's surface is covered by water?

2) What is the intertidal zone?

3) What causes waves?

CHALLENGE: What are the three largest seas in the world?

Card #8

SCIENCE

Would you recognize an arachnid if you saw one? If you've ever seen a spider, then you know what an arachnid looks like. Learn more about spiders and other arachnids by browsing through this site:

Spiders

http://sciencebulletins.amnh.org/biobulletin/biobulletin/story991.html

1) Aside from spiders, what animals belong to the arachnid family?

2) About how many known species of spiders are there?

3) What is the world's largest spider?

CHALLENGE: What is a scientist who studies spiders called?

Card #5

SCIENCE

Clouds create beautiful sculptures across the blue sky. Did you know that a cloud's size, shape, and height can tell meteorologists a lot about the weather? Learn more about clouds and meteorology at the following site:

Meteorology Program: Cloud Boutique

http://vortex.plymouth.edu/clouds.html

1) How far up is a cloud that is considered high?

2) What type of cloud produces heavy rain, lightning, thunder, hail, and strong winds?

3) What are lens-shaped clouds called? How are they formed?

CHALLENGE: How do meteorologists generally classify clouds?

Card #7

Card #6

Answers:

1. 870,000 miles or 1,392,000 kilometers
2. 88 Earth days
3. Atmospheric scientist

CHALLENGE: Nucleus

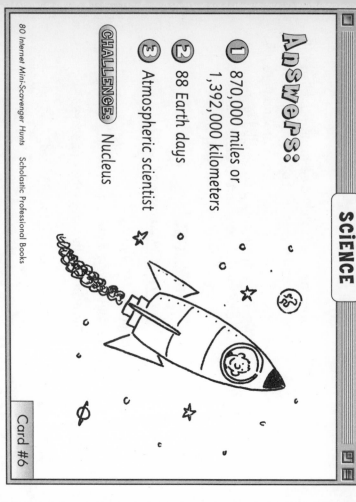

Card #8

Answers:

1. $\frac{3}{4}$ of the earth's surface
2. The area exposed between high and low tides
3. Wind

CHALLENGE: South China Sea, Caribbean Sea, Mediterranean Sea

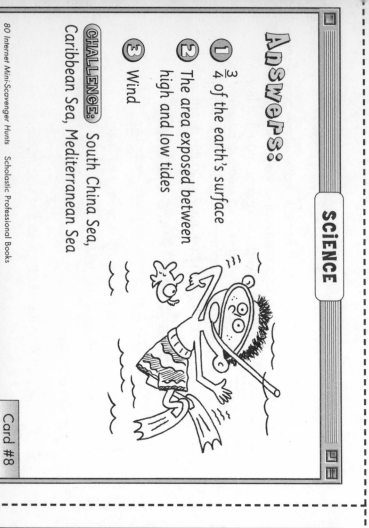

Card #5

Answers:

1. Scorpions, ticks, mites, daddy longlegs
2. 36,000 species
3. Giant bird-eating spider

CHALLENGE: Arachnologist

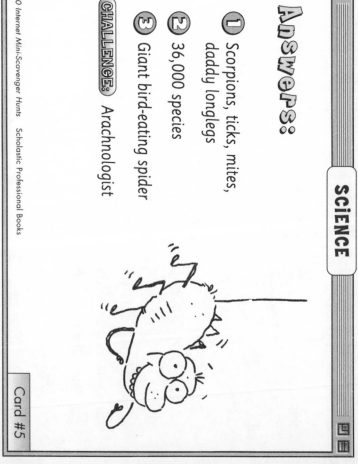

Card #7

Answers:

1. Cloud's base above 18,000 feet
2. Cumulonimbus
3. Lenticular clouds are formed from strong wind flow over rugged terrain.

CHALLENGE: By their altitude, appearance, and origin

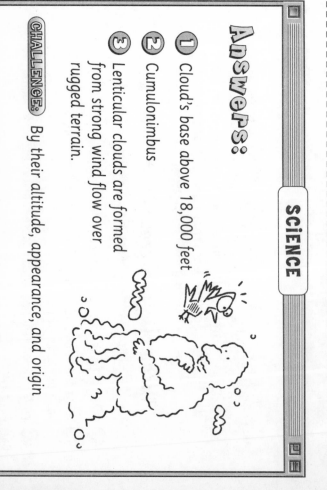

SCIENCE

The Earth is our only home, and we must learn to take better care of it. Explore the links in this Web site to learn about pollution, the greenhouse effect, and other vital environmental issues. Then answer the questions below:

EduGreen

http://edugreen.teri.res.in

1) What is the greenhouse effect?
2) What is smog?
3) What are three types of solid waste?

CHALLENGE: Create a list of ways that you and your classmates could work together to save the planet.

Card #10

SCIENCE

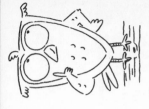

Owls are unique and fascinating creatures with a distinct lifestyle. What makes these mysterious creatures of the night so captivating? Find out at the following Web site, then answer the questions below:

The Owl Pages

http://www.owlpages.com/physiology/Default.htm

1) What is a group of owls called?
2) How many eggs does a female owl lay?
3) What is the only continent where you can't find owls?

CHALLENGE: Owls are birds of prey. What does this mean?

Card #12

SCIENCE

Coral reefs are among the most amazing sights in the ocean! Thousands of species of fish and plants make their home in the reefs. Amaze your friends with the awesome facts you will find at this site:

Sea World: Coral Reefs

http://www.seaworld.org/infobooks/coral/coralcr.html

1) What is the largest barrier reef in the world? How large is it?
2) What is the initial source of energy for coral reefs?
3) What are the three types of reefs?

CHALLENGE: How does deforestation on land affect coral reefs underwater?

Card #9

SCIENCE

Did you know that our world is divided into biomes or communities? Each biome has its own specific plant and animal life that have adapted to their particular environment. Explore Earth's different biomes by clicking on this Web site:

The World's Biomes

http://www.ucmp.berkeley.edu/glossary/gloss5/biome

1) What are the two basic regions of the aquatic biome?
2) How much of the earth is covered by deserts?
3) What's the difference between the Arctic tundra and the Alpine tundra?

CHALLENGE: Why are aquatic biomes considered the most important of all biomes?

Card #11

Card #12

Answers:

1. Parliament
2. 1 to 13 (average is around 3 or 4)
3. Antarctica

CHALLENGE: They hunt other animals for food.

Card #10

1. The effect caused when gases such as carbon dioxide, methane, and nitrous oxide trap solar radiation from escaping the atmosphere, keeping the Earth warm
2. Water molecules mixed with dust and smoke particles, forming a dense fog
3. Municipal waste, hazardous waste, and infectious waste

CHALLENGE: Answers will vary.

Card #11

Answers:

1. Freshwater and marine
2. $\frac{1}{5}$ of the earth's surface
3. The Arctic tundra encircles the north pole and extends south to the coniferous forests of the taiga. The Alpine tundra is found on mountains at high altitudes where trees can't grow.

CHALLENGE: Water is a major natural resource, and is the basis of life.

Card #9

Answers:

1. Great Barrier Reef, which stretches more than 1,240 miles
2. The sun
3. Fringing reef, barrier reef, and atoll

CHALLENGE: When forests are cut down, topsoil washes into rivers and into the sea. The soil smothers coral polyps and blocks sunlight, which corals need to survive.

SCiENCE

Are you brave enough to fly into the eye of a hurricane? When conditions are favorable for hurricane development, Hurricane Hunters fly into the eye of the hurricane to determine its precise location, motion, strength, and size. Join their adventures at:

Hurricane Hunters

http://www.hurricanehunters.com

1. What division of the U.S. armed services do the Hurricane Hunters belong to?
2. During a mission, how many times might the Hurricane Hunters fly into the eye of a hurricane?
3. Which hurricane was called "the perfect storm"?

CHALLENGE: Where are the Hurricane Hunters based?

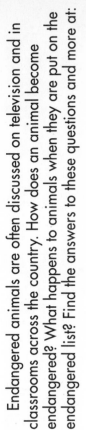

Card #14

SCiENCE

Endangered animals are often discussed on television and in classrooms across the country. How does an animal become endangered? What happens to animals when they are put on the endangered list? Find the answers to these questions and more at:

Endangered Species Information

http://endangered.fws.gov/wildlife.html

1. What is an endangered species?
2. What is a threatened species?
3. About how many species of animals and plants in the United States are listed as threatened and endangered?

CHALLENGE: Why was the American alligator removed from the endangered species list?

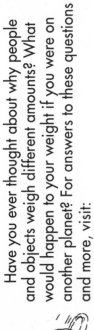

Card #16

SCiENCE

Did you know that the average adult heart weighs only about 11 ounces? That same heart will beat more than two and a half BILLION times, without pausing, in a lifetime. Learn all about the human heart at this site:

The Heart: An Online Exploration

http://sln.fi.edu/biosci/heart.html

1. What fruit does the heart resemble?
2. How much blood flows through an average adult's body?
3. List three things you can do to keep your heart healthy.

CHALLENGE: Why is blood considered to be alive?

Card #13

SCiENCE

Have you ever thought about why people and objects weigh different amounts? What would happen to your weight if you were on another planet? For answers to these questions and more, visit:

Your Weight on Other Worlds

http://www.exploratorium.edu/ronh/weight

1. What is mass?
2. Define weight.
3. What is the relationship between the force of gravity and distance?

CHALLENGE: Find your weight on Mercury, Jupiter, the sun, and the moon.

Card #15

Card #16

Answers:

1. An endangered species is in danger of extinction throughout all or a significant portion of its range.

2. A threatened species is likely to become endangered in the foreseeable future.

3. 517 species of animals and 745 species of plants

CHALLENGE: It has fully recovered.

Card #16

Card #14

Answers:

1. Air Force

2. Four, if they have enough fuel

3. Hurricane Grace

CHALLENGE: Keesler Air Force Base in Biloxi, Mississippi

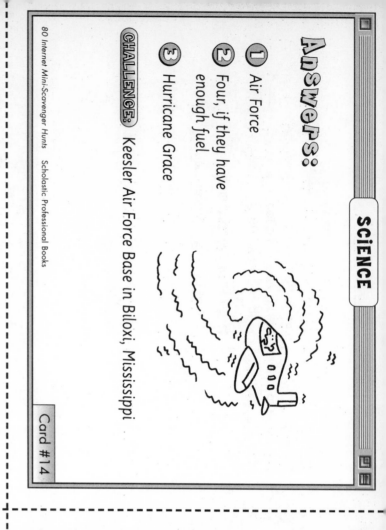

Card #14

Card #15

Answers:

1. The amount of matter an object contains

2. Weight is the measure of the force of attraction or pull of gravity between two objects (such as you and the Earth).

3. The force of gravity gets weaker with distance. It decreases with the square of the distance.

CHALLENGE: Answers will vary.

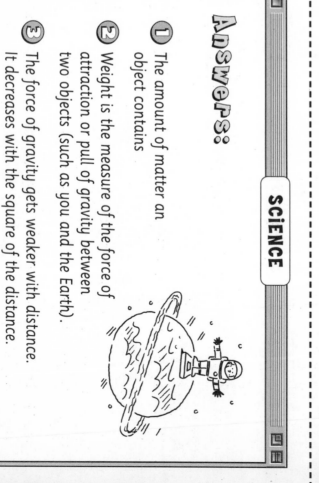

Card #15

Card #13

Answers:

1. An upside-down pear

2. 5 liters

3. Get plenty of exercise, follow a good diet, and stay drug-free

CHALLENGE: Because it contains living cells

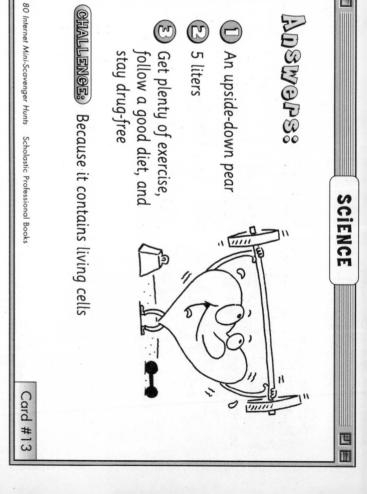

Card #13

As the Earth's only natural satellite, the moon inspires a lot of questions. How did the moon come to be? Why does it change shape throughout the month? Explore the following site to find a wealth of interesting information about our moon:

To the Moon

http://www.pbs.org/wgbh/nova/tothemoon

1. Who was the last man on the moon?
2. How many days does it take for the moon to orbit the earth?
3. Who was the first scientist to see the moon's features and how?

CHALLENGE: What is the "Big Three"?

Card #18

Think work is hard? Ever tried to lift, pull, or move a heavy object? What can make such work easier? Simple machines. Visit this site to learn a few tips for making simple machines work for you:

Simple Machines

http://sln.fi.edu/qa97/spotlight3/spotlight3.html

1. Name the six simple machines.
2. What simple machine are you using when you try to pry a nail out of a board with a hammer?
3. What is a compound machine?

CHALLENGE: What is work?

Card #20

If you have ever dug around in the dirt, you've probably discovered an earthworm or two. What good are earthworms to our environment? What do they eat? How long can they get? These questions and many more can be answered when you visit:

Adventures of Herman the Earthworm

http://www.urbanext.uiuc.edu/worms/index.html

1. How did the earthworm arrive in North America?
2. How many hearts does an earthworm have?
3. What organ helps the earthworm grind its food to tiny pieces?

CHALLENGE: What class of animals does the earthworm belong to?

Card #17

Does light have a color? If so, what color is it? How do you see the color of light? Enlighten yourself by browsing through the following site, then search for the answers to the questions below:

Colors of Light

http://www.mhschool.com/student/science/mhscience/
5/review/summary/5-3-6.html

1. What is a prism?
2. When your retina is struck with red light and green light, what color do you see?
3. What do you call the band of colors produced when light passes through a prism?

CHALLENGE: What color does a green leaf not absorb?

Card #19

Card #18

SCIENCE

Answers:

1. Eugene Cernan

2. 29.5 days

3. Galileo through his spyglass

CHALLENGE: The three main theories of how the moon came to be (The moon was a chunk of Earth that was flung off during our planet's early years; the moon was a small planet that got caught in Earth's gravity; the moon was formed independently and side by side with the Earth)

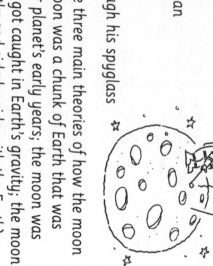

Card #18

Card #20

SCIENCE

Answers:

1. Inclined plane, wedge, pulley, screw, wheel and axle, and lever

2. Lever

3. Two or more simple machines that work together

CHALLENGE: A force acting on an object to move it across a distance

Card #20

Card #17

SCIENCE

Answers:

1. Through early European settlers who brought plants to North America in the 1600s and 1700s. Earthworms were hidden in the soil among the plants' roots.

2. 5

3. Gizzard

CHALLENGE: Oligochaeti

Card #17

Card #19

SCIENCE

Answers:

1. A piece of glass or plastic shaped like a triangle and spreads colors by refraction

2. Yellow

3. Spectrum

CHALLENGE: Green

Card #19

Card #2

Your principal has promised to replace your classroom's ratty carpet if the class can figure out exactly how much carpet is needed. To help you find the area of your classroom, check out this site:

Geometry

http://pittsford.monroe.edu/jefferson/calfieri/geometry/geoframe.html

1. If your classroom floor is shaped like a rectangle, what two measurements do you need to find its area?

2. Say your class is 30 feet long and 20 feet wide. How many square feet of carpet do you need?

3. The classroom next door is 28 feet long and 25 feet wide. What is its area?

CHALLENGE: Find the area of your own classroom.

Card #2

Card #4

In a "magic square" the numbers in each row, column, and diagonal add up to the same sum. Check out this site to help you fill in the magic square below:

All Math

http://www.allmath.com/magicsquare.asp

Fill in this magic square with the numbers 1 to 9 so that each row, column, and diagonal adds up to 15.

			=15
			=15
			=15

=15 =15 =15 =15

CHALLENGE: Create your own magic square to solve.

Card #4

Card #1

Fred could very well be a professional basketball player when he gets older. At 16 years old, he's already 72 inches tall! His younger sister, Mary, is not far behind. She's 68 inches tall. Use the Web site below to convert their heights from inches to feet:

Math Cats Convert Numbers

http://www.mathcats.com/explore/convert.html

1. What are Fred's and Mary's heights in feet?

2. Find the sum of their heights in inches.

3. Now convert your answer in #2 to feet.

CHALLENGE: It's exactly six miles from your house to the library. How many feet would you have to walk to the library and back home?

Card #1

Card #3

What can be more fun and challenging than a brainteaser? Use this Web site to help you figure out the answer to the puzzle below:

A Simple Calculator

http://www.maths.utas.edu.au/People/Michael/Calculator.html

Write the numbers 1 to 9 in descending order (9, 8, 7, 6, 5, 4, 3, 2, 1) on a piece of paper. Place seven plus signs (+) between the numbers to create an equation that totals 99. Which two numbers did you have to group together?

(NOTE: If you don't get the correct answer the first time, simply click the "Back" button on your browser and rearrange the plus signs.)

CHALLENGE: Write the numbers 9 to 1 again. This time, find a sum that equals 99 using only six plus signs.

Card #3

Card #2

Answers:

1. Length and width
2. 600 square feet
3. 700 square feet

CHALLENGE: Answers will vary.

Card #4

Answers:

6	7	2
1	5	9
8	3	4

CHALLENGE: Answers will vary.

Card #1

Answers:

1. Fred is 6 feet tall and Mary is 5.666667 feet tall.
2. 140 inches
3. 11.66667 feet

CHALLENGE: 63,360 feet

Card #3

Answers:

$$9 + 8 + 7 + 65 + 4 + 3 + 2 + 1 = 99$$

CHALLENGE: $9 + 8 + 7 + 6 + 5 + 43 + 21 = 99$

Your school is holding its first annual geometry bee. You have one week to master geometric operations. Visit this site to train to become a geometric master:

Geometry

http://pittsford.monroe.edu/jefferson/calfieri/geometry/geoframe.html

1. How many faces does a cylinder have? How many vertices?
2. List three types of quadrilaterals.
3. What is the formula for finding the volume of a rectangle?

CHALLENGE: A triangle has a length of 10 and a height of 20. What is its area?

Card #6

0, 1, 2, 3, 4, 5, 6, 7, 8, 9… These 10 digits are the basis for the mathematical system (also known as the decimal or base-10 system) we use every day. But did you know that we also use a binary number system? Find out more when you visit this site:

Binary System

http://www.usbyte.com/common/Binary%20System.htm

1. How many digits are used in a binary number system? What are they?
2. Where is the binary number system used?
3. What is the binary equivalent of 14?

CHALLENGE: In the binary system, what is 1 + 1?

Card #8

Can you run a kilometer? Do you know how far a kilometer is? Do the words *centimeters, decimeters,* and *kilometers* sound like a foreign language to you? Go to the following site to get in tune with metric measurement, then solve the problems below:

Converting Metric Length Units

http://www.aaamath.com/mea69-metric-meter.html

1. While on vacation, you learn that the beach is 5 kilometers from your hotel. Convert that distance to meters.
2. How many meters are in a decimeter?
3. The sign on the pool says it is 3 meters deep. How many centimeters deep is the pool?

CHALLENGE: How many hectometers are in a kilometer?

Card #5

Roman numerals were the standard numbering system in Europe and Rome until 900 A.D. Imagine having to add, subtract, or multiply X's and V's. Go to this site to learn more about Roman numerals, and then answer the questions below:

Legion XXIV Roman Numerals

http://www.legionxxiv.org/numerals

1. Which number is there no Roman numeral for?
2. What number does the Roman numeral L represent?
3. What does placing a smaller value before a larger value indicate?

CHALLENGE: What does a Roman numeral with a bar above it represent? Give the value for X and $\overline{X}$.

Card #7

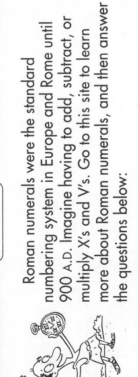

Card #8

MATH

Answers:

1. Two; 1 and 0
2. Computer science and technology
3. 01110

CHALLENGE: 10

Card #8

Card #6

MATH

Answers:

1. 2 faces, 0 vertices
2. Rectangle, square, trapezoid, parallelogram, rhombus
3. Length x height x width

CHALLENGE: 100

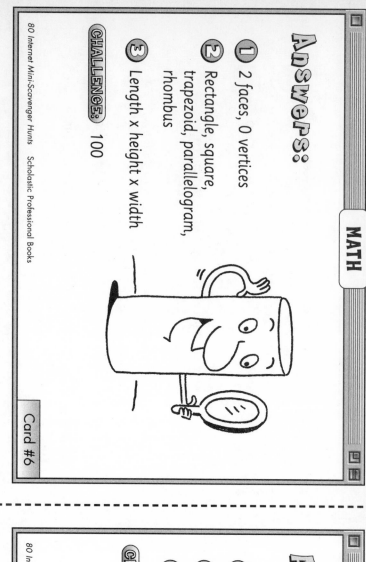

Card #6

Card #7

MATH

Answers:

1. 0
2. 50
3. Subtraction

CHALLENGE: The Roman numeral's value is multiplied by a thousand. X = 10; $\overline{X}$ = 10,000

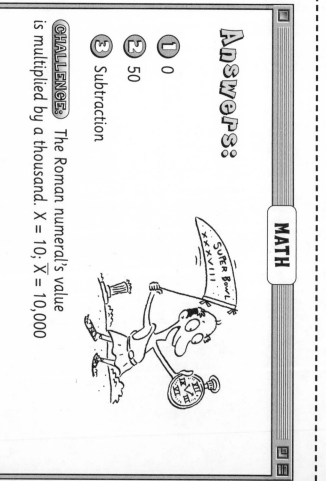

Card #7

Card #5

MATH

Answers:

1. 5,000 meters
2. $\frac{1}{10}$ of a meter
3. 300 centimeters

CHALLENGE: 10

Card #5

MATH

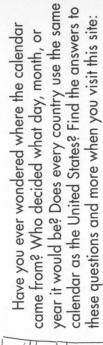

Do you check the temperature before deciding what you'll wear or do each day? You may be surprised to know that temperature is not just about the weather. Browse through this site to learn more:

About Temperature

http://www.unidata.ucar.edu/staff/blynds/tmp.html

1. What is the boiling temperature of water in Fahrenheit?
2. Who created the first mercury thermometer in 1724?
3. Convert 28 degrees Celsius to Fahrenheit.

CHALLENGE: What is the formula for converting Celsius to Kelvin?

Card #9

MATH

Have you ever wondered where the calendar came from? Who decided what day, month, or year it would be? Does every country use the same calendar as the United States? Find the answers to these questions and more when you visit this site:

It's All About Time

http://www.timechange.com/3m

1. Who developed the calendar system we use today?
2. Before 1752, on what date did England celebrate the New Year?
3. Where was the name February derived?

CHALLENGE: In 1986, new rules were established for Daylight Saving Time in the United States. List the two points made in this legislation.

Card #10

MATH

I refuse to be positive!

Your early math years focused on adding, subtracting, multiplying, and dividing positive numbers. Today your teacher introduced numbers that are less than zero—negative numbers! Visit this site to learn the rules of positive and negative numbers, then solve the problems below:

Positive and Negative Numbers

http://pittsford.monroe.edu/jefferson/calfieri/algebra/PosNeg.html

1. $-456 + -45 =$
2. $-364 + 16 =$
3. $-23 \times 6 =$
4. $-34 \times -3 =$

CHALLENGE: Mathematicians determined a correct order of operations. List the order.

Card #11

MATH

Algebra may sound daunting, but it's fun once you learn and work through its rules and operations. Visit the following Web site for easy-to-understand answers to some of algebra's most difficult questions:

Introduction to Algebra

http://www.mathleague.com/help/algebra/algebra.htm

1. What is a variable?
2. Label these three number sentences as equations or expressions:

   $2 + y + 7$ $(3 + 9) \times 6 - 3$ $24 + 7 = 33$
3. Solve for x: $8x = 168$

CHALLENGE: List the proper operation for each key word: sum, product, difference, quotient.

Card #12

Card #10 (MATH)

Answers:

1. Pope Gregory XIII
2. March 25
3. Februar, the Roman festival of purification

CHALLENGE: Daylight Saving Time begins at 2:00 A.M. on the first Sunday in April and ends at 2:00 A.M. on the last Sunday in October.

Card #10

Card #12 (MATH)

Answers:

1. A symbol that represents a number
2. Expression, expression, equation
3. 21

CHALLENGE: Addition, multiplication, subtraction, division

Card #12

Card #9 (MATH)

Answers:

1. 212 degrees
2. Gabriel Fahrenheit
3. 82.4 degrees Fahrenheit

CHALLENGE: K = °Celsius + 273

Card #9

Card #11 (MATH)

Answers:

1. –501
2. –348
3. –138
4. 102

CHALLENGE: Parentheses, exponents, multiplication, division, addition, subtraction

I refuse to be positive!

Card #11

"Money makes the world go 'round," or so the saying goes. It's certainly hard to imagine what our world would be like without money. How much do you know about money? Explore this Web site to learn some interesting facts:

Making Scents of Money

http://library.thinkquest.org/J003358F

1. When was the last time a $1,000 bill was printed?
2. Name the two cities in our country where currency is printed.
3. When was the U.S. Mint established and by whom?

CHALLENGE: What is a penny made of?

Card #13

In first grade, place value meant hundreds, tens, and ones. Now that you're older, place value goes all the way up to billions. The great news is that there is a pattern to place value and, with a little practice, place value becomes easy. Learn more at the following site:

All About Place Value

http://www.aaamath.com/plc.html

1. What place value does 8 hold in the number 486,754?
2. How much is 6 worth in the number 26,857?
3. Write 327,654 in the expanded form.

CHALLENGE: What is the place value of 6 in the number 0.7286?

Card #14

Graphs, charts, and tables are great ways to illustrate a concept when words are just not enough to explain it. To discover how to use and read charts, graphs, and tables, look through this site. Then answer the questions below:

Tables and Graphs

http://cstl.syr.edu/fipse/TabBar/Contents.htm

1. What is a cell?
2. What does the table title explain?
3. What does each sector of a circle graph represent?

CHALLENGE: Take a survey of your classmates' favorite food, color, or band, and create a graph to show the results.

Card #15

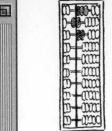

You've probably learned about our nation's history. But what about the history of numbers and mathematics? Explore this site to learn more about the rich history of mathematics. Then answer the questions below:

Mathematics History Topics Index

http://www-groups.dcs.st-andrews.ac.uk/~history/
Indexes/HistoryTopics.html

1. Where did early math originate?
2. In the Mayan numeral system, how is the number 5 represented?
3. When did the number zero first appear in Indian mathematics?

CHALLENGE: How did the Babylonians divide the day, hour, and minute?

Card #16

Card #16

Answers:

1. Babylonia
2. —
3. 650 A.D.

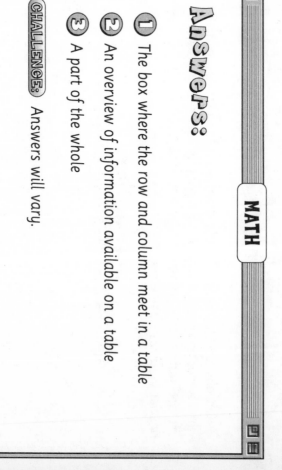

CHALLENGE: 24 hours in a day, 60 minutes in an hour, and 60 seconds in a minute

---

Card #14

Answers:

1. Ten-thousands place
2. 6,000
3. 300,000 + 20,000 + 7,000 + 600 + 50 + 4

CHALLENGE: Ten-thousandths

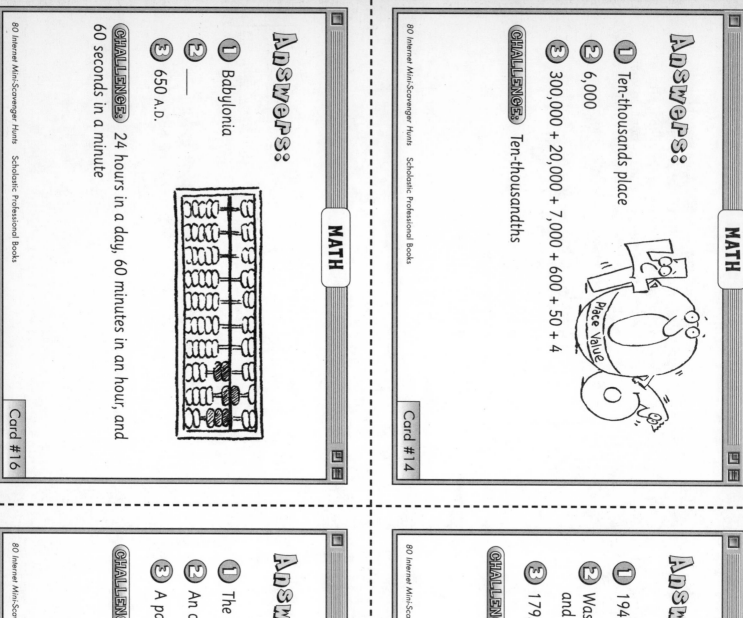

Card #15

Answers:

1. The box where the row and column meet in a table
2. An overview of information available on a table
3. A part of the whole

CHALLENGE: Answers will vary.

Card #13

Answers:

1. 1946
2. Washington, D.C., and Fort Worth, Texas
3. 1792 by Congress

CHALLENGE: Copper-plated zinc

True, you must learn your multiplication facts! But did you know that there are easier ways of learning facts than just by memorization alone? Check out this great site with tons of tricks and techniques for learning and brushing up on your multiplication facts:

Multiplication: An Adventure in Number Sense

http://www.naturalmath.com/mult

1 What is the commutative law of multiplication?

2 Give a rule for multiplying numbers (up to 9) by 11.

3 Use the trick for multiplying a number by 5 to solve these problems:

12 x 5 =   9 x 5 =   14 x 5 =   22 x 5 =

CHALLENGE: 12,345 x 10 =

Card #18

Our country's measurement system is different from that of most other countries in the world. Most countries use the metric system, while the United States uses the standard system. Learn how to convert between the two systems at this site:

Metric Conversion Table

http://convert.french-property.co.uk

1 How many yards are in a mile?

2 How many centimeters are in 8 inches?

3 How many meters are in a yard?

CHALLENGE: On your family vacation, your dad says that you'll be traveling 240 miles. How many feet is that?

Card #20

Mathematics is more than just addition, subtraction, multiplication, and division. It has theories, laws, principles, and more. Once you learn the rules and meanings to this game we call math, it is easier and a lot more fun to play! Visit this site to begin the fun:

The Golden Ratio

http://library.thinkquest.org/C005449/glossary.html

1 What is a golden triangle?

2 What is the difference between an equilateral triangle and an isosceles triangle?

3 Define the term axiom.

CHALLENGE: The golden ratio, also known as phi, has what value?

Card #17

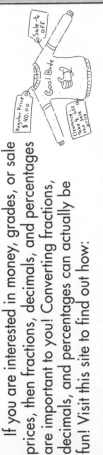

If you are interested in money, grades, or sale prices, then fractions, decimals, and percentages are important to you! Converting fractions, decimals, and percentages can actually be fun! Visit this site to find out how:

Math Forum: Fractions, Decimals, & Percentages

http://mathforum.org/dr.math/faq/faq.fractions.html

1 Give the formula for converting fractions to decimals.

2 How do you convert fractions to percentages?

3 Convert this fraction to a decimal and to a percent: $\frac{3}{8}$

CHALLENGE: Convert this decimal to a fraction: 3.5

Card #19

Card #18

Answers:

1. A x B = B x A

2. When multiplying by 11, simply double the number, e.g. 11 x 8 = 88

3. 60, 45, 70, 110

CHALLENGE: 123,450

Card #20

Answers:

1. 1,760 yards

2. 20.32 centimeters

3. 0.9144 meters

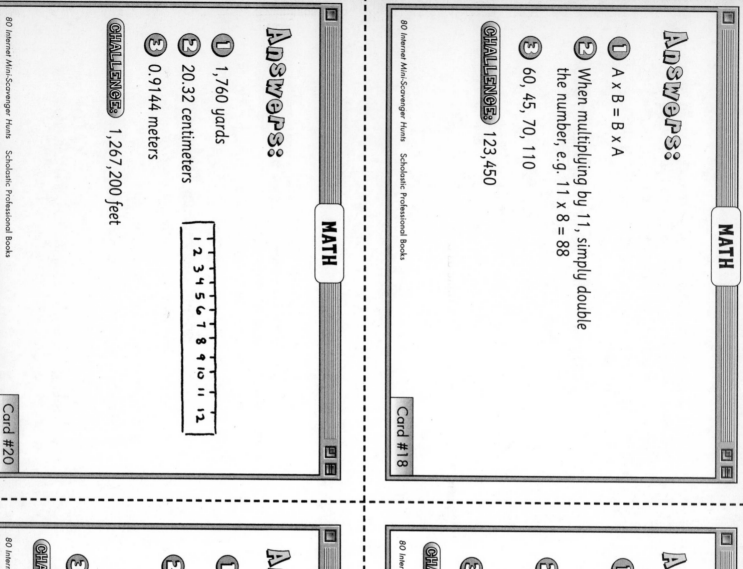

CHALLENGE: 1,267,200 feet

Card #17

Answers:

1. An isosceles triangle with base angles of 72 degrees and a vertex angle of 36 degrees

2. An equilateral triangle has all sides congruent, while an isosceles triangle has at least two sides that are congruent.

3. A universally recognized truth

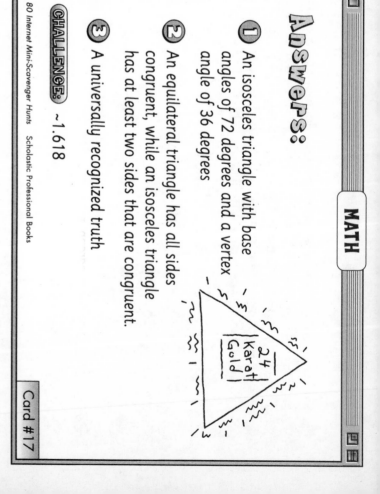

CHALLENGE: ~1.618

Card #19

Answers:

1. Divide the numerator by the denominator.

2. Divide the numerator by the denominator, then move the decimal point two places to the right.

3. 0.375, 37.5%

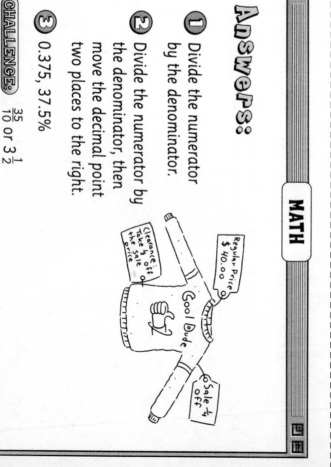

CHALLENGE: $\frac{35}{10}$ or $3\frac{1}{2}$

It's your first week back from vacation, and your first homework assignment asks you to find the main idea of a story. The summer months have fogged your memory. What exactly is the main idea? Visit this Web site to find out:

The Main Idea

http://www.manatee.k12.fl.us/sites/elementary/palmasola/rcmi1.htm

1. What is a main idea?
2. What part of a paragraph often tells you the main idea?
3. Where else in a paragraph might an author state the main idea?

CHALLENGE: Write a paragraph, then challenge classmates to find the main idea.

Card #1

How many times have you heard your teacher say, "Use active voice!"? What is active voice? How does it make your writing better? Scroll down this Web site to learn more about writing and the benefits of active voice:

Rules of Usage

http://www.bartleby.com/141/strunk5.html#11

Use the active voice to rewrite these sentences:

1. Our Thanksgiving dinner was eaten by the dog.
2. The reason she withdrew from the tennis match was because of her hurt ankle.
3. The news that he lost came as a surprise to everyone.

CHALLENGE: Write two sentences, first using the passive voice, then changing it to the active voice.

Card #2

Ancient Greek dramatists like Sophocles had an enormous influence on the literature and plays we read today. Greek tragedies are especially captivating once you understand the language. Learn more about Sophocles and Greek dramas by visiting this site:

Rivendell's Drama Page – Sophocles

http://www.watson.org/%7Eleigh/drama.html#sophocles

1. Where and when was Sophocles born?
2. How long did Sophocles live?
3. Other than a dramatist, what occupation did Sophocles hold?

CHALLENGE: Though Sophocles wrote well over 100 plays, only seven have remained intact. List those seven.

Card #3

Long before *The Lord of the Rings* became a series of high-grossing movies, it was a best-selling series of fantasy books by J. R. R. Tolkien. It was published in three parts between 1954–1955. Learn more at the following site:

J. R. R. Tolkien: A Biographical Sketch

http://www.tolkiensociety.org/tolkien/biography.html

1. What do the initials J. R. R. stand for?
2. What book was the prequel to The Lord of the Rings?
3. What post did Tolkien hold in 1925?

CHALLENGE: What book written by Tolkien was published after his death?

Card #4

Answers:

Answers may vary, but could include the following:

1. The dog ate our Thanksgiving dinner.
2. She withdrew from the tennis match because she hurt her ankle.
3. Everyone was surprised that he lost.

CHALLENGE: Answers will vary.

Card #2

Answers:

1. John Ronald Reuel
2. The Hobbit
3. The Rawlinson and Bosworth Professorship of Anglo-Saxon at Oxford University

CHALLENGE: The Silmarillion

Card #4

Answers:

1. The main reason the story was written
2. Topic sentence
3. The last sentence

CHALLENGE: Answers will vary.

Card #1

Answers:

1. Athens, Greece, in 496 B.C.
2. 90 years
3. Politician

CHALLENGE: Ajax, Antigone, The Women of Trachis, Oedipus the King, Electra, Philoctetes, and Oedipus at Colonus

Card #3

LANGUAGE ARTS

Your class is debating whether to use a comma or semicolon when joining two independent clauses. Do you remember the rule? Review the rule of joining independent clauses at the site below:

Rules of Usage

http://www.bartleby.com/141/strunk.html#5

Write a rule about independent clauses that your classmates are sure to understand.

CHALLENGE: Under what conditions would it be acceptable for two independent clauses to be separated by a comma?

Card #5

LANGUAGE ARTS

Katherine Paterson is the award-winning author of *Bridge to Terabithia, The Great Gilly Hopkins,* and many more books. Her books are full of adventure and excitement, as well as colorful and emotional characters. Explore the following site to learn more about her life and work:

Bridge to Terabithia

http://www.terabithia.com

1. Who does Katherine Paterson say was her greatest influence?
2. What inspired her to write Bridge to Terabithia?
3. For which books did Paterson win Newbery awards?

CHALLENGE: What did Katherine Paterson want to be when she was a child?

Card #6

LANGUAGE ARTS

Where would you go if you needed help spelling a word, pronouncing a word, or finding a word's meaning? The dictionary, of course! Try out this online version:

Visit Merriam-Webster Online

http://www.m-w.com/netdict.htm

1. Look up the word pendulum. Write the second definition for this word.
2. Find contrasting words for the adjective kind.
3. What are synonyms for the word impatient?

CHALLENGE: As what parts of speech can the word pretty be used?

Card #7

LANGUAGE ARTS

Did you know that Spanish is the second-most commonly spoken language in the United States? More than 17 million people in the U.S. speak the language. Become acquainted with Spanish by visiting:

Learn Spanish

http://www.studyspanish.com/freesite.htm

1. List the cardinal numbers 5 to 10 in Spanish.
2. Write the following words in Spanish: horse, sheep, and donkey.
3. Translate the phrase: "Good morning! How are you?"

CHALLENGE: How is the letter "a" pronounced in Spanish?

Card #8

Card #6

Answers:

1. Her husband

2. Her son's best friend died when she was struck by lightning.

3. The Great Gilly Hopkins, Jacob Have I Loved, and Bridge to Terabithia

CHALLENGE: A movie star or a missionary

Card #5

Answers:

Join independent clauses using a semicolon, not a comma. Another correct way to use two independent clauses in a sentence is to create two separate sentences.

CHALLENGE: When the clauses are joined by a conjunction, such as and, a comma is permissible. It is also acceptable to use a comma between clauses if they are short and alike in form.

Card #8

Answers:

1. Cinco, seis, siete, ocho, nueve, diez

2. El caballo, la oveja, el burro

3. ¡Buenos días! ¿Cómo está usted?

CHALLENGE: Short /a/ (like the /a/ in father)

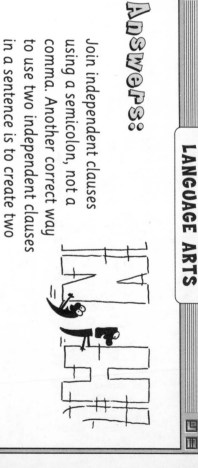

hola!

Card #7

Answers:

1. Something that alternates between opposites

2. Cruel, fierce, inhuman, savage, harsh, grim, implacable, merciless, unrelenting

3. Chafing, fretful, unpatient, unforbearing, unindulgent, eager, agog, anxious, appetent, ardent, athirst, avid, breathless, keen, thirsty

CHALLENGE: Adjective, adverb, noun, transitive verb

LANGUAGE ARTS

Although prepositional phrases may not be on top of your list of favorite topics, they are an important part of the English language. Find out how you can identify these phrases by browsing through this site:

Big Dog's Grammar

http://aliscot.com/bigdog/prepositions.htm

Identify the prepositional phrases in the following sentences:

1. After the test, I drove to town.
2. Jan, Lucy, and Tracy gave their friends necklaces to thank them.
3. The kids set up their tents under the tree.

CHALLENGE: Brainstorm as many prepositional phrases as you can think of in 60 seconds.

Card #10

LANGUAGE ARTS

Louisa May Alcott, one of the greatest authors of the 19th century, wrote more than a dozen books, several poems, and many essays. Even though she died more than 100 years ago, her books remain on the best-seller list. Find out more about this talented author at:

Alcott Web

http://www.alcottweb.com

1. When was Louisa May Alcott born?
2. What is the title of her most famous book?
3. Name the poem she wrote at the death of her mother.

CHALLENGE: What connection does Louisa May Alcott have with space?

Card #12

LANGUAGE ARTS

You've been assigned to read a Caldecott book. What exactly is a Caldecott book? How does a book become one? Explore the following Web site to find out:

The Caldecott Medal

http://www.ala.org/alsc/caldecott.html

1. Who gets awarded the Caldecott Medal each year?
2. Who is the Caldecott Medal named after?
3. What is the Caldecott Medal made out of?

CHALLENGE: What book received the first Caldecott Medal, and in what year?

Card #9

LANGUAGE ARTS

The Capitol is in the capital.

English is a very confusing language. When do you use *there* instead of *their*, or *your* instead of *you're*? It would be easier to remember if English just made sense! Visit this site, which is dedicated to solving the mysteries surrounding the English language:

Common Errors in English

http://www.wsu.edu/~brians/errors

1. What is the difference between an anecdote and an antidote?
2. Write two sentences, one using capitol and the other capital.
3. What parts of speech are the words good and well?

CHALLENGE: Use the words to, too, and two correctly in one sentence.

Card #11

LANGUAGE ARTS — Card #10

Answers:

1. After the test
2. to thank them
3. under the tree

CHALLENGE: Answers will vary.

LANGUAGE ARTS — Card #12

Answers:

1. November 29, 1832
2. Little Women
3. "Transfiguration"

CHALLENGE: A crater on Venus is named after her

LANGUAGE ARTS — Card #9

Answers:

1. The artist of the most distinguished American picture book for children
2. Randolph J. Caldecott, a 19th-century English illustrator
3. Bronze

CHALLENGE: Animals of the Bible, A Picture Book in 1938

Picture Book

LANGUAGE ARTS — Card #11

Answers:

1. An anecdote is a humorous story or a tale. An antidote is a remedy against poison.
2. Sentences will vary, but capitol should refer to a building, while capital refers to cities and all other uses.
3. Good is an adjective (describes a noun) and well is an adverb (describes a verb, adjective, or another adverb).

CHALLENGE: Answers will vary.

LANGUAGE ARTS

Freckle Juice, Blubber, and *Tales of a Fourth Grade Nothing* are just a few of the wonderful books written by Judy Blume. Her books are so delightful that they are just as much fun to read the second time around. Discover more about this great author by visiting:

Judy Blume's Official Website

http://www.judyblume.com

1. Where did Judy Blume attend college?
2. What were her favorite books when she was growing up?
3. Where is her favorite place to write?

CHALLENGE: Who is Peter Hatcher's mischievous little brother?

Card #13

LANGUAGE ARTS

American literature blossomed in the 19th century during the time known as the American Renaissance. A large part of that growth can be attributed to Ralph Waldo Emerson. To learn more about this great writer's life and work, visit:

Ralph Waldo Emerson

http://www.pbs.org/wnet/ihas/poet/emerson.html

1. What did Ralph Waldo Emerson prefer to be called?
2. What was the name of the first major essay he published?
3. What were Ralph Waldo Emerson's three careers?

CHALLENGE: What did Emerson's friends do when his house of 37 years burned down?

Card #14

LANGUAGE ARTS

Has a teacher ever criticized your handwriting as "too messy"? Neat handwriting isn't an easy skill to develop. With practice, your handwriting will get better over time. Visit this site to learn great tips on improving your cursive handwriting:

Rules for Good Handwriting

http://www.argonet.co.uk/users/quilljar/rules.html

1. Where should small letters start?
2. Describe how down strokes should be written.
3. Name a fact about ascending and descending letters.

CHALLENGE: What does the word cursive mean?

Card #15

LANGUAGE ARTS

Harry Potter. What kid hasn't heard of his name? The Harry Potter craze has swept the nation and even the world. Everyone, from children to adults, loves his books. Learn more about Harry Potter and his adventures at this site:

Hogwarts Online

http://library.thinkquest.org/C006090/index_e.html

1. Who is the author of the Harry Potter books?
2. What is Ron Weasley's relationship with Harry Potter? How many siblings does Ron Weasley have?
3. When is Harry Potter's birthday?

CHALLENGE: How many years did it take for the author to write the first Harry Potter book?

Card #16

Card #14

Answers:

1. Waldo
2. "Nature"
3. Preacher, poet, philosopher

CHALLENGE: His friends rebuilt his home for him while he traveled abroad.

Card #16

Answers:

1. J.K. Rowling
2. Ron Weasley is Harry Potter's best friend. He has five brothers and one sister.
3. July 31

CHALLENGE: 5 years

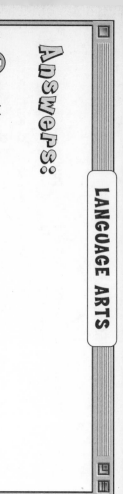

Card #13

Answers:

1. New York University
2. The Betsy-Tacy series by Maud Hart Lovelace
3. In a tiny cabin on an island that she goes to every summer

CHALLENGE: Fudge

Card #15

Answers:

1. At the top
2. Down strokes should be written parallel.
3. Ascending and descending letters should be no more than twice the height of small letters.

CHALLENGE: Joined up or joined together

You know you have to study to get good grades. But sometimes, it can be so hard! Looking for some helpful study hints? Check out this Web site, then answer the questions below:

Study Skills

http://www.how-to-study.com

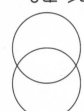

1) Why do you need a clock when you are studying?
2) Name four health tips that will improve study habits.
3) Where should you try to sit in all of your classes? Why?

CHALLENGE: What does PQR3 stand for?

Card #17

Your teacher suggested you use a graphic organizer to compare and contrast your two favorite books. What is a graphic organizer? How would you use it to compare and contrast your two favorite books? Find out more at this site:

Compare and Contrast: Graphic Organizers

http://www.writedesignonline.com/organizers

1) What is one common trait shared by graphic organizers?
2) Name a graphic organizer that you can use for comparing and contrasting.
3) Define the word contrast.

CHALLENGE: Use one of the three graphic organizers to compare and contrast your two favorite books.

Card #18

Jean Craighead George's love of nature is apparent in many of her books, including the award-winning *Julie of the Wolves*. She has written more than 100 books and has won more than 20 awards. Visit this site to learn more about Jean Craighead George and her books:

Jean Craighead George

http://www.jeancraigheadgeorge.com

1) Aside from Julie of the Wolves, what other book by Jean Craighead George won the Newbery Medal?
2) What are the names of her three children?
3) What are the titles of the two sequels to Julie of the Wolves?

CHALLENGE: What inspired her to write My Side of the Mountain?

Card #19

Holes, Out of the Dust, and *Maniac Magee.* What do these books have in common? They've all won the Newbery Medal. What is the Newbery Medal? How does a book win this award? Learn more at:

Newbery Medal Home Page

http://www.ala.org/alsc/newbery.html

1) Who is the Newbery Medal named after?
2) What year was the Newbery Medal first awarded?
3) What association awards this medal?

CHALLENGE: What book received the Newbery Medal in 1986?

Card #20

Card #18

Answers:

1. They show the order and completeness of a student's thought process
2. Venn diagram, T-chart, compare/contrast matrix
3. To compare two or more things, especially to show their differences

CHALLENGE: Answers will vary.

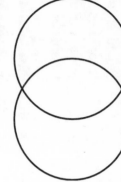

Card #20

Answers:

1. 18th-century British bookseller John Newbery
2. 1922
3. American Library Association

CHALLENGE: Sarah, Plain and Tall

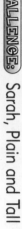

Card #17

Answers:

1. To help you manage your time
2. Get enough sleep, eat three good meals a day, exercise, and take frequent study breaks
3. Near the front of the class. You can usually listen better if you are near the front.

CHALLENGE: Preview, question, read, recite, and review

Card #19

Answers:

1. My Side of the Mountain
2. Twig, Craig, and Luke
3. Julie and Julie's Wolf Pack

CHALLENGE: Her family's trips to the wilderness along the Potomac River near Washington, D.C.

Notes

Notes